ANYTIME ANYWHERE, ANYBODY GAMES

by Andrea DiNoto
illustrated by Marina Givotovsky

gb GOLDEN PRESS · NEW YORK
Western Publishing Company, Inc.
Racine, Wisconsin

Created and Produced by Tree Communications, Inc., New York
Managing Editor: J. Munves, Art Director: M. E. Gold
Design Assistants: T. Augusta, C. F. Jones

Table of Contents

Let's Play

Let's play, let's play. What's a good game for today? Do you feel like sitting quietly to play a thinking game? Or is it just the day for running and playing a game of tag or a relay race? How many games do you know without even looking inside the pages of this book? Lots and lots probably. But have you ever taught yourself a game? You can, you know. In this book there are almost 40 games and you can teach yourself to play as many as you want just by reading each one carefully and following the instructions.

As you go through the book, you might find that some of the games are too easy for you. But there are many others to choose from. There are games for one and two people, circle games, running games, brain games, and more. Some require equipment like a ball, paper and pencil, balloons, or some rope. But for most of them all you need is yourself and some friends to play with.

Who Goes First?

In many games, someone must be chosen to go first. If there are only two players, you can flip a coin to see who it will be. First, each player chooses **heads** or **tails**. Suppose you choose **heads**. If you flip the coin and it lands **heads up**, you go first. If it lands **tails up**, the other person goes first.

Choosing Up Sides

In some team games, like tag and relay races, the people who play must be divided into two equal groups. This is easy to do if everyone stands in a line and counts off.

To do this, the first in line says "One." The next says "Two" and so on until everyone has said a number. The odd numbers make up one team and the even numbers are the other.

Choosing Who Is IT

In many games, one player is **IT**. Being **IT** means that you must do something different from all the others, like tagging them, or finding them if they are hiding, or making a guess about what they are doing.

There are lots of ways to choose **IT**. The easiest and quickest way is for the players to call out "Not **IT**!" as soon as they decide on a game to play. The last one to call "Not **IT**!" is **IT**.

Drawing Straws

A quieter way of choosing **IT** is to draw straws. These can be real pieces of straw, paper soda straws, or strips of paper. If you are holding the straws, have one for each player (including yourself), but break or cut one shorter than the others. Hold the straws so they all look the same length. Let everyone draw a straw. The one who picks the short straw is **IT**.

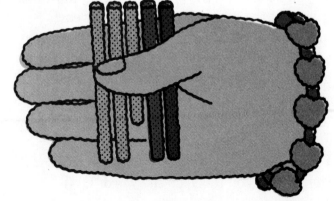

One-Potato, Two-Potato

Do you know **One-Potato, Two-Potato** and **Engine, Engine, Number Nine**? They are rhymes that have been chanted for years and years. If you say them with hand motions, they become games for deciding who is **IT**. For this, the players sit in a circle with their fists in the center. If you are the leader, you touch each fist with your own as you go around the circle, chanting the rhyme at the same time. Touch a fist each time you say a word. Begin with yourself by touching your chin, then your other fist. Continue around the circle to the other players and as you go say,

"One potato, two potato, three potato, Four, Five potato, six potato, seven potato, More. Y-O-U spells YOU and O-U-T spells OUT." The person you touch on the word "OUT" must put his fist behind his back before you go around again. The last person with a fist in the circle is **IT**.

You can do the same thing with this rhyme:

Engine, engine, number nine
Coming down the Chicago line
If the train should jump the track
Would you want your money back?

The player whose fist you touch on the word **back** must answer "Yes" or "No." After he answers, continue by saying, "Y-E-S spells YES and O-U-T spells OUT," or "N-O spells NO and O-U-T spells OUT." Again you will land on a fist on the word "OUT" and that player must put that fist behind his back. Go round and round, repeating the rhymes until all but one player is eliminated. That player is **IT**.

Finger Call

It is easy to win a guessing game like Finger Call, but only with a little bit of luck. And if more than two people play, you will find that it is even more difficult to make a lucky guess.

To start, the players face each other. Each puts one hand behind his back and makes a fist with the other. At a given signal, like a nod of the head, each holds out any number of fingers he wants from the hand with the fist. At the same time, and before all the fingers are out, everyone must shout out his guess as to how many fingers there will

be. A player does not have to hold out any fingers if he does not want to, but he can hold out all five. So, if only two hands are in the game, you can guess any number from zero to ten. (The highest number you can guess is equal to five times the total number of hands in the game.)

Call out your guesses loud and clear. Play the game fast, but check each time to see if anyone has made the right guess. Score one point for each correct guess. The first person to score five points wins.

Pebble Tossing

If there is no one around to play with, it is a good time to practice tossing and throwing. That will improve your aim and help you play a better game when someone else comes along. You can play this game indoors or out. All you need is a handful of pebbles and a stone that is larger than the rest. Stand about 6 feet (2 meters) from the stone and toss the pebbles at it, one at a time. See how close you can get each pebble to the stone. Give yourself one point every time you hit the stone with a pebble.

When you think you are a pretty good shot, challenge someone to a game. When you play this way, take turns tossing. If your pebble lands closer to the stone than your opponent's does, you get a point. If his comes closer, he scores a point. If both pebbles seem to be the same distance from the stone, use a tape measure to determine who came closest.

The first person to score 15 points wins the game.

Three-Box Throw

One or two or more can play Three-Box Throw. To play, you will need three boxes of different sizes like the ones shown here. Put the boxes inside each other so that the smallest is in the middle and the biggest is outside. Be sure there is at least a 4-inch (10-cm) space between the boxes. Then glue them together, and put the Three-Box on the floor. Standing 3 yards (3 meters) away, toss beans or pebbles into it. The bull's-eye is three points, the middle box counts as two points, and the outside box is one point. If you play by yourself, see how fast you can score ten points. If you play with someone else, take turns tossing. The first one to score ten points wins.

Wastebasket Basketball

You can play this game alone in your room on a rainy day or with a friend. It is another one that helps you improve your aim. You will need an empty wastepaper basket, or a pot or pail. Make a ball by crumpling up a piece of paper, like a paper napkin or a sheet of newspaper. Tape the paper with cellophane tape so it doesn't come undone. Now you are ready to play. To start, stand 10 feet (3 meters) from the basket, and throw the ball as if you were throwing a real basketball. See if you can get the ball into the basket ten times in a row. If you can, make the game a little harder by using a paper coffee cup instead of a wastepaper basket. Tape the cup to a door, about 6 feet (2 meters) from the floor. As you can see, it is much harder to get the ball into the cup. You can give yourself one point each time you make a basket, or score yourself this way: Make your first shot. If you make the basket, score one point. If you miss, take a second shot from the spot where the ball fell. If you get the second shot in the cup, add another point to your score. If you miss, take a third shot from where the ball landed. If you get it in, add on another point. If you miss, the game is over. Add up your points. With this type of scoring, the lower the score, the better. If two people play, alternate shots, using the same ball. Low score wins.

Race Horses

With some string and cardboard, you can have a horse race around a sturdy table leg. Kitchen or playroom tables are best. They usually have metal legs that can't be cut or scratched. To make the horses you will need some tracing paper, a pencil, and scissors. Each player makes his own horse. First trace the horse below on tracing paper and cut it out along the outlines. Lay the tracing-paper horse on a piece of cardboard and trace around it. Cut out the cardboard horse and punch a small hole in it where the dot is, using the pointed tip of the scissors.

Cut a 1-yard (1-meter) long piece of string for each horse that will be in the race. All strings must be the same length. Tie one end of each string to a table leg. Thread the other ends through the horses. For the race, every player holds a string, pulling it tight. (Be sure that all the horses are the same distance from the table leg.) When someone says "GO!" each player tugs, jerks, and snaps the string to make his horse move down to the table leg. The player who reaches the end of the line first is the winner.

Do-Not-Laugh Games

Can you keep a straight face? Can you NOT smile and NOT laugh at something funny? Here are two games that will put you to the test.

Ha Ha

At least six people should play this game to make it funny. Have everyone sit in a circle. Count off so that everyone knows his number. The first person says "HA!" The second says "HA! HA!" The third says "HA! HA! HA!" and so on, all around the circle. Anyone who laughs, smiles, or makes a mistake is out of the game. The HA HAs must be said very quickly as you go around so that no one has much time to think.

Poor Kitty

In Poor Kitty, the person who is **IT** is the Kitty (or Doggy or Piggy, if you like). **IT** must go to each person in the game and kneel down and make a very sorrowful animal noise. A Kitty must meow. A Doggy must whine. A Piggy must oink. The idea is that Kitty must try to make someone laugh.

The person that Kitty kneels to must pat him on the head and say "Poor Kitty" (or "Poor Doggy" or Poor Piggy"). But he must not laugh. If he does not laugh, Kitty goes to someone else. If he does laugh, that person is out and becomes the new Kitty.

Sardines

This is a good hide-and-seek game to play in a house that has lots of small places to hide in. It is also a good game to play at a party where there are lots of people. Someone is chosen to be **IT**. He is the first Sardine. While all the other players close their eyes and count to fifty, he finds a hiding place. When the other players finish counting, they all go to look for him. The first one to find the Sardine hides along with him and stays very still and quiet. One by one, as each person finds the Sardine's hiding place, they squeeze in and hide there, too. When everybody is packed together like sardines in a can, the game is over.

The one who first found the original Sardine is the Sardine for the next game.

Button Button

You may know this game by the name of Thimble Thimble. To play, you will need one small object that can be held and hidden in the hand, like a button or a thimble. One player is **IT** and has the button. The others sit in a circle with their hands cupped behind them. The player with the button walks around the outside of the circle and pretends to put the button into the hands of each player, and each player pretends to take it. One player really does get the button, but he doesn't let the others know. Everyone sitting in the circle watches closely to see if they can tell who has received the button. Sometimes the one who has the button looks very guilty or smiles too much. After **IT** has walked around once he stands in the middle and says, "Button, Button, Who has the button?" The people in the circle call out their guesses one by one. The one who makes the correct guess is the next button passer.

Hot Potato

Hot Potato is one of the oldest and simplest games in the world and lots of fun to play. You will need a beanbag or a ball to be the "hot potato." All players should stand or sit in a circle. One person, chosen to be the leader, starts the game by throwing the "potato" to one of the players. The leader then turns his back to the circle so he cannot watch the action. Imagine the beanbag or ball to be a very, very hot potato and you won't want to hold on to it for long. Pass it quickly by throwing it to another person. Keep it moving until the leader shouts "STOP!" Anyone caught holding the potato at that moment is out. Keep going around until there is only one player left, the winner.

Kitty Wants a Corner

To play Kitty Wants a Corner, get five people together—yourself and four friends—and find a room with four corners and very little furniture. Choose one player to be the Kitty. The others stand in the corners of the room. Whoever is Kitty must go up to each player and plead, "Kitty Wants a Corner." Each shakes his head "NO!" Kitty then stands in the middle of the room and says again, "Kitty Wants a Corner!" Now the other players must run and change corners, and Kitty tries to steal a corner while they are running. Anyone left without a corner is the new Kitty in the middle.

Cat and Mouse

Play this game with at least eight people. Let one be the Cat and one be the Mouse. The rest should join hands and form a circle. The Cat chases the Mouse around the circle. The others should help the Mouse escape by raising their arms to let him in and out of the circle. They can try to keep the Cat out by lowering their arms. Of course, the Mouse always gets caught anyway in this game. When that happens, the Cat becomes the new Mouse, a new Cat is chosen, and the old Mouse joins the circle.

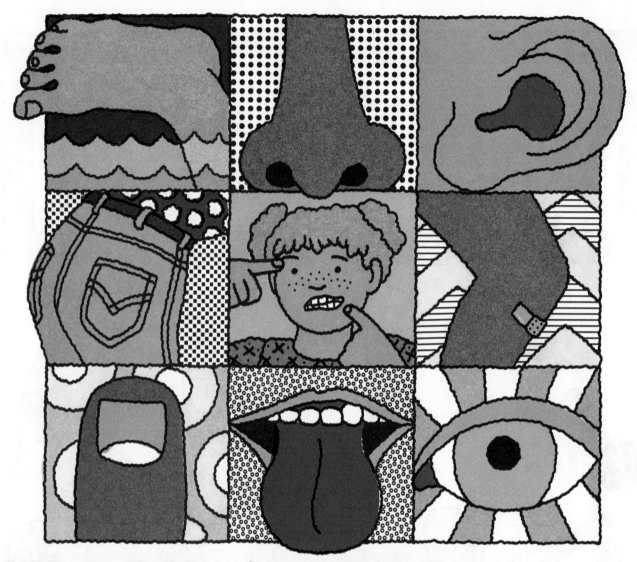

Mixed-Up Anatomy

Have you ever mistaken your chin for your nose? In this crazy game you might—if you're not careful. To start, one person is chosen as the leader. He stands in front of the group and begins the game by tapping his nose and saying, "Nose, Nose, Mouth." When he says "Mouth," he taps some other part of his body, like his ear or knee. The other players must do as he says, not as he does. The idea is for the leader to trick the other players into following his movements. Anyone who makes the wrong movement is out.

Continue playing, using different parts of the body. For example:
"Chin, Chin, Knee" (if you are the leader, say **knee** and touch your head or arm).
"Arm, Arm, Ear" (say **ear** and touch your nose).

The last player to be eliminated wins and is the new leader.

Japanese Tag

Japanese Tag is another mixed-up anatomy game, with a twist. It should be played outdoors with lots of people and lots of space. In this game, the person who is **IT** tries to tap someone in a silly spot, like their knee or elbow or the top of the head. The person tagged must then hold that spot with one hand while he runs and tries to tag someone else. A tagged player can go back to his normal position only after he tags someone else. The game can go on for as long as you like, since it ends only when everyone gets tired of running around.

Catch the Dragon's Tail

Dragon's Tail is an unusual kind of tag game because all the players hold on to each other as they run. The players form a dragon by standing in a line with their hands on each other's shoulders. As the dragon runs around, twisting and turning, the Head, or first person in line, tries to tag the last person, who is the Tail. When the Head succeeds in tagging the Tail, he goes to the end of the line, and the next person in the line becomes the new Head. The game is over when everyone has had a turn as Head and Tail.

22

12 O'Clock Midnight

For 12 o'Clock Midnight, you need one Wolf, a lot of Sheep, and a big outdoor area where there is plenty of room to run. It should not be too hard to find one mean Wolf among your playmates. The others can be the Sheep. The Wolf chooses an area for his den, and the Sheep choose a spot for their pen. The two places should be a good distance from each other. At first the Wolf stays in his den and the Sheep stay in their pen. The game begins when the Sheep and Wolf come wandering out. Any Sheep can come as close as he dares to the Wolf to ask the time.

"What time is it, Mr. Wolf?" The Wolf may answer any time he chooses, "1 o'clock, 2 o'clock, 3 o'clock . . . " A Sheep knows that it is safe to be roaming about if the Wolf answers any time but "12 o'Clock Midnight." When he says that, the Sheep must run for safety because the Wolf will try to tag them. Any Sheep tagged before he reaches the safety of his pen is taken away by the Wolf. He must then help the Wolf catch the other Sheep. When all the Sheep have been tagged the game is over and a new Wolf is chosen.

Sleeping Monster

If you have younger brothers and sisters, or if you sometimes baby-sit for young children, they will love to play this game with you. Gather together lots of small objects that can be the Monster's treasure. Announce that you are a Monster and that you would like to take a nap. Say that if you wake up and catch anyone moving or trying to steal any of your treasures, you will become very angry and chase them and put them in your dinner pot. For this game your dinner pot could be a chair or sofa. Spread your treasure all around you and lie down and pretend to sleep. The others will then creep up and try to snatch the treasure away. The Monster must wake up suddenly and try to catch anyone who is moving. If he does, they are put in the dinner pot and are out of the game. Do this until everyone has been caught. The last one to be caught is the winner and becomes the new Sleeping Monster.

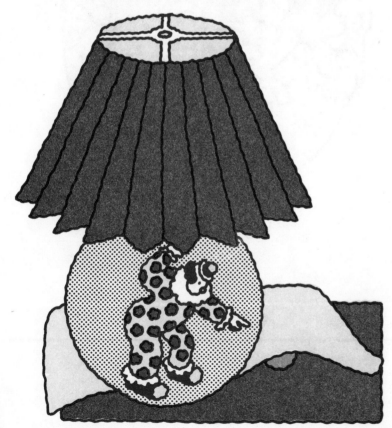

Hot and Cold

The whole family can play this game indoors with you. All you need is a thimble or other small object and one person to be **IT**. Have **IT** leave the room while you hide the object. Hide it well but where it can still be seen — between the slats of a venetian blind or behind a lamp, for example. Now let the person who left the room come back and look for the object. If he comes close to it, you and all the other players cry "Warm." If he comes very close you say "Hot," and if he comes very, very close, you say "Burning hot." Of course, if he wanders away from it, you cry, "Cold, very cold, ice cold." Once **IT** discovers the object, he becomes one of the players, and another **IT** or searcher is chosen. Everyone should take turns being the searcher.

Tapping

In Hot and Cold, the person who is **IT** has to find an object. In Tapping, **IT** must discover an action that the group wants him to perform. As in Hot and Cold, **IT** leaves the room while the others decide on something that they want him to do. They may want him to open the window, turn off a light, or pick up a rug. When **IT** comes back, he walks around the room. If he comes close to the thing on which he is to perform the action, the others make loud tapping sounds. If he wanders away, they tap very softly. In this way, the players guide **IT** toward the place and the action. **IT** should keep in constant motion, trying to discover what he is to do, touching things and listening to the tapping to see if he is getting Hot or Cold. When he discovers and performs his action, a new **IT** is chosen.

Barnyard

Barnyard is a very fine game to play when you are in a story-telling mood. You need to know or be able to make up a funny story about animals in a barnyard. It can be any story at all so long as the names of lots of animals are mentioned often. For example, a good story would include a chicken, rooster, donkey, cow, dog, cat, pig, horse, wolf, bird, and any other creature that makes a familiar noise. Assign an animal to each player. Explain that each time you mention an animal, the person you assigned it to must make the appropriate noise—squawk for a chicken, bark for a dog, moo for a cow, and so on. If you cannot invent a story, look for one to read aloud. This can be a very funny, very noisy game.

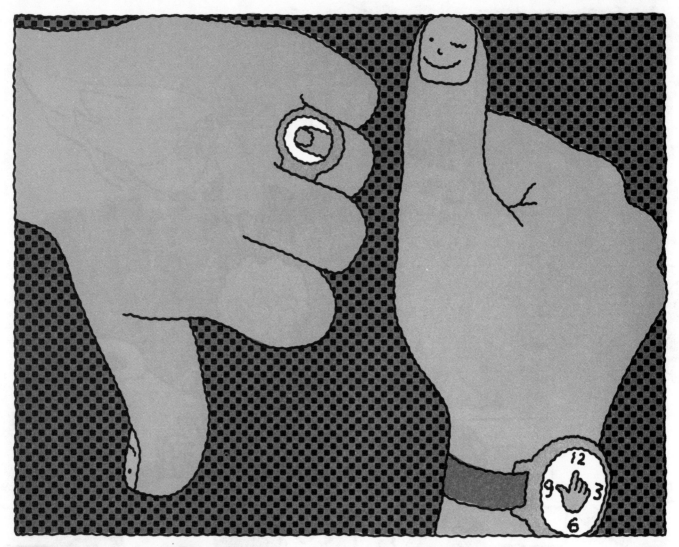

Harry Says

Have you ever played Simon Says? In that game all the players follow the movements of a leader as long as he says "Simon Says" before giving the command. Harry Says is like Simon Says, but when you play it you only move your thumbs. Sit on the floor with one or more friends. Decide who will be the leader. Make fists with your thumbs sticking up. The leader begins by giving commands like "Harry says thumbs up; Harry says thumbs down." Follow the leader's command, turning your thumbs up or down with him **only if he says a name first**. The leader can say any name to confuse you. He can say, "Harry says" . . . or "Judy says" . . . or "Bobby says" . . . or "Sally says . . . thumbs up." If the leader gives the command with no name, you must not move or you will be out of the game. If you are the leader, speak very quickly and try to confuse the other player or players. Anyone who follows ten commands correctly wins and becomes the new leader.

The Secret Leader

It is easy to tell who is leading the band when the conductor stands up front. But suppose he were hidden among the musicians? Do you think you could detect who was leading the band then? In this game, the leader is hidden among the players and if you are **IT**, you must discover who the leader is just by watching everybody's actions. At least ten people should play this game to make it interesting.

One player is **IT** and leaves the room. The others sit in a circle. One person in the circle is chosen to be the Secret Leader. He must start and lead all the movements without drawing attention to himself. The other players follow him without seeming to look at him and without giving away his identity.

The leader should think of movements that have good rhythms, like clapping, snapping fingers, bobbing the head, rolling the eyes, making mouth sounds. The rhythm should not be broken when the movements change.

As the movements start, **IT** should come back. If you are **IT**, stand in the middle of the circle and observe everyone's movements very closely. If you think you know who the leader is, call out the name. If that person is not the leader, he will simply shake his head **NO**, and continue to follow the Secret Leader without breaking his rhythm. When you guess the Secret Leader correctly, the Secret Leader becomes **IT**, a new Secret Leader is chosen, and you become one of the players.

Tug Tied

This game, which is really a test of strength, is like a mixed-up tug of war. You will need three or more pieces of strong rope like clothesline or jump-rope cord. Choose pieces that are all the same length. Knot them together at one end, as the picture shows. Tug hard on the ropes to make sure the knot is strong and tight. Lay the ropes on the ground with the knot in the center and the ropes coming out from it like wheel spokes. Six feet (2 meters) from the end of each rope, place a small object, like a toy or rock. Each object should be far enough from the rope so that you have to stretch to touch both at the same time.

For the game the players pick up their rope ends and pull hard like in a tug of war. Each tries to reach and pick up his object while preventing the others from reaching theirs. The one who tugs the hardest will pull the others off balance and reach his object first.

Jump the Shot

You have to be fast on your feet for Jump the Shot. The shot is a towel tied to the end of a long rope. One player, the twirler, holds the shot. The other players stand and form a circle around him. They should stand at least 6 feet (2 meters) apart. The twirler can stand and bend over, sit, or even lie down in the center. He twirls the shot around himself. It should swing at ankle height of each player in the circle. The jumpers must pay attention and keep watching the shot so they can jump over it when it swings around to them. They may not move back to escape it. Anyone who misses and stops the shot, or who steps back, is out. The last person out wins.

If the twirler stands up to twirl the shot, he might get a little dizzy. If this happens, stop the game and let someone else twirl.

Trample

You play this zany balloon game with your feet, so everyone must wear sneakers. Use very large balloons if possible, and have two balloons for each player. Start by marking out a large chalk circle on the pavement or a playroom floor. Do not mark circles on rugs or carpets or good wood floors. Next, all players tie a balloon to each ankle with string. (Tie the balloons just tight-ly enough so they rest on the ground near your feet when you are standing still.) All players enter the circle. When the signal is given, each player tries to step on and burst everyone else's balloons while keeping his own from being broken. This requires fast thinking and faster moving. Crying over stepped-on toes is not allowed.

Balloon Relay

Balloon Relay is especially good to play at parties. Each team will need a blown-up balloon and a piece of cardboard. The game starts like this: Once all the furniture is cleared out of the way of the racers, the team members form two lines behind a starting line which can be a piece of string laid out on the floor or an imaginary line. Again, do not mark lines on rugs, carpets, or good floors. The first player on each team is given the balloon and cardboard. At the signal, the racers fan the balloons to a goal line 15 feet (5 meters) away, and back again. Each hands the cardboard to the next person on his team, who repeats the action. The players may not tap or push the balloon with the cardboard. They must move it just by flapping the cardboard to create a wind behind it. The first team to complete the race wins.

East and West

In East and West, two teams of players form lines facing each other. One line is East and the other is West. There should be at least 15 feet (5 meters) between the two lines. One side is chosen to go first and that side sends out one player. If you are that player, you go to the opposite team, where all the players are holding their hands out, palms up. Go down the line from one player to the next, gently stroking their hands. But whenever you feel ready to run like crazy, instead of stroking a player's hand, slap it. Then try to race back to your team without being tagged. If the slapped player is able to chase and tag you, you must go back and become part of his team. If not, the player you slapped becomes part of your team. Then the team you went to sends out a player and repeats the action. East and West keep taking turns until one side has accumulated most of the players.

Hop-It Relay Race

To play in this race, you must be able to hop while holding a volleyball or other large ball between your knees. This is not easy to do if your legs are not long enough. Sometimes a bit of practice before starting the game is helpful. Divide your group into two teams with the same number of players. Each team gets a ball and forms a line behind the starting line. The first player in each team holds the ball behind his back and, at the starting signal, runs to a far line about 50 feet (15 meters) away. Once he reaches that line, he stops, puts the ball between his knees, and hops back to the starting line. Then he hands the ball to the next player on his team, who does the same thing. If the ball falls at any time, the player must retrieve it, put it back between his legs, and continue hopping. Walking or waddling with the ball is not allowed. Each player on each team must hop the ball back to the starting line. The team that finishes first wins.

Quick-Change Relay

Worn out grownups' clothes—old baggy pants, funny hats and shoes, dresses, gloves, and coats—can be found in almost everyone's house. Gather together as much as you can find for this game. (But get permission first. What looks worn out to you may not look that way to someone else.)

Since this game is a relay race, divide the players into two teams. Make a pile of old clothes for each team and put the two piles in boxes or bags at one end of the room you are playing in. Each box should contain the same **number** of things to wear but not necessarily the same **kind** of things.

The teams line up behind a piece of string or any other starting line, which should be across the room from the boxes of clothes. At the signal "GO!" the first player from each team runs to his team's box and puts on all the clothes in the box. All buttons must be buttoned; all shoes must be laced; all belts must be buckled. When the players are dressed, each runs back to his team, takes everything off, and gives the clothes to the next player. That player must put on the clothes and run back to the box and take them off again. Then he runs back to his team and tags the next player, and the next player runs to the box to put the clothes on again. Whew! The game continues this way until every member from one team has put on and taken off the clothes. That team wins.

38

crunch
crunch

bibble
bibble

tweet
tweet

crackle
sizzle

Hidden Noises

The leader of this game gathers all sorts of material and objects with which to make strange or familiar sounds. All these things must be hidden from the other players who will be asked to guess at what they are hearing. The objects can be hidden behind a large piece of cardboard or a curtain made from a towel or sheet. As the players sit with pencil and paper, the leader calls out "Number 1," makes the noise, and gives the players time to write down their guesses. He keeps his own list with the correct answers. At the end, the person with the most correct answers wins.

When you are the leader, you might want to make interesting noises by crumpling cellophane; tearing sheets of newspaper; tapping a bottle; crunching a cracker; dropping a coin into a glass of water. These are only a few suggestions. See how many more you can think of. The noises can be more varied and more interesting if you use a tape recorder. Record the sounds of a creaking gate, pots and pans, birds, animals, traffic, bacon frying, and a hundred other things. Keep track of each thing you record and number it both on the tape and on a written list. For example, before recording the chirping of a bird, say "Number 1" into the recorder but do not say what the sound is. Note it down instead on a piece of paper. This way, you will always know the sounds you have recorded without giving them away.

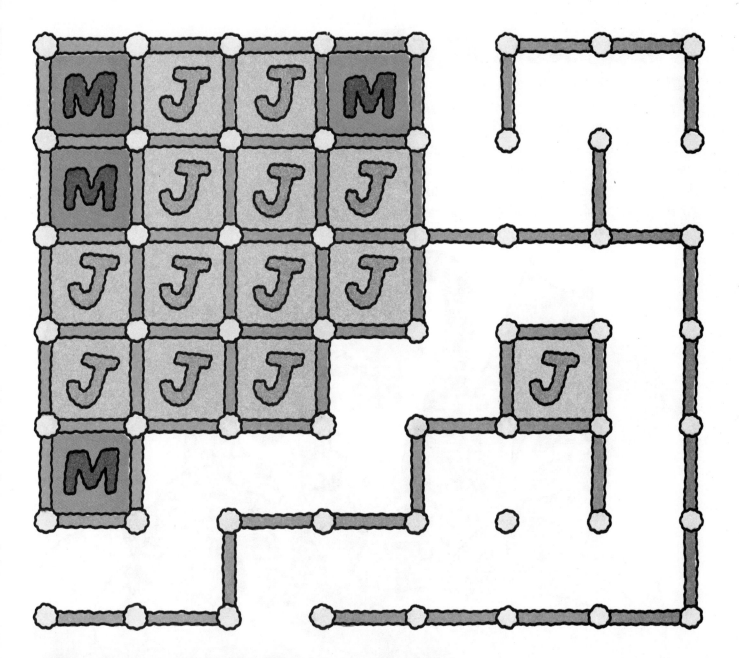

Dots and Squares

Paper and pencil are needed for this game for two or more players. First draw a square of dots. To make the lines of dots even, use lined paper and a ruler. The square can be as small as seven dots down and seven across, or as large as you like.

Players take turns connecting the dots with pencil lines to form boxes. Every time someone forms a box he puts his initials inside. The person who fills the most boxes with his initials wins.

I Packed My Bag

This game is sometimes called "I Took a Trip." It is a memory game that you can play anywhere: at a party, during a long car trip, or with a friend on a rainy day. Start the game by saying "I packed my bag and in it I put a . . . . " Here, say anything you like: a book, a hat, a shoe. The next person repeats what you have said and adds something to the list. Each person must repeat the list and add another object. As the list gets longer and longer, it gets harder to remember all the things that have been packed in the bag and what the right order is. The game goes on until no one can repeat the entire list without a mistake.

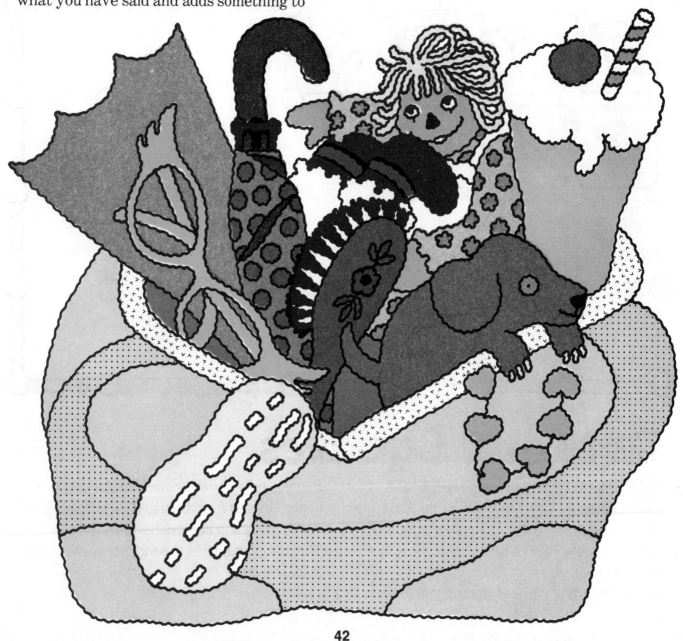

Ghost

All word games require quick thinking, and **GHOST** is no exception. It is a spelling game in which you try not to be the person who makes a word. The first time a person makes a word, he gets a **G**. The next time he gets an **H**, the third time he gets an **O**, and so on. Once a person gets all the letters in the word **GHOST**, he is out of the game.

Suppose you are the first player. Think of a word and say the first letter. If your word is **ANGRY**, you would say **A**. The second player must add a letter to **A** that does **not** make a word. For example, if he adds a **T** (**AT**) or an **N** (**AN**) he has formed a word and he gets a **G**. He may add the letter **B** if he has the word **ABSENT** in mind, and he **must** have a word in mind, as you will see. The third player must add another letter that does not form a word. He may add an **A**. If the fourth player suspects that there is no word that begins **ABA**, he can challenge the player who added the **A** by saying, "What word are you thinking of?" If the third player can show that there is a word that begins **ABA**, the fourth player loses his challenge and gets a **G**. If the third player cannot show that there is a real word that begins **ABA**, **he** loses the challenge and gets a **G**. In this case, the fourth player would get a **G** because the third player was thinking of **ABACUS**. Each time a player completes a word or loses a challenge, he acquires another letter of the word **GHOST**.

When it is your turn, if there is no other choice but to finish a word, you must do so. But most of the time, you can get out of that by thinking of a new word. For example, when it's your turn, you may have to deal with the letters **FAM**. If you add an **E**, you form **FAME** and get a letter. But if you think of a new word, like **FAMILY**, you can add the **I** and not form a word.

Do not use proper names or three-letter words, which are too easy to complete. Brush up on your vocabulary if you plan to win at **GHOST**.

1. I am thinking of the word apple. A....

2. Maybe the word is angry. N.... whoops! <u>An</u> is a word!

3. That's right! If you make a word, you get a letter from Ghost. You get a G.

4. Now we start over with a new word. I'm thinking of the word stone. S....

Spot It

Car games can be a lot of fun, and they are fine as long as you don't annoy the driver. This one is a contest to see who can spot the most things from his side of the car. Decide what you want to spot and give points for each thing. For example, a certain kind of animal, like a squirrel, could be worth five points; out-of-state license plates could be three points; green cars could be one point. There is just one rule—you may look out of the window only on your side of the car. Every time you see one of the objects that has been agreed upon, call it out and give yourself the right number of points. Give yourself points each time you spot it. Twenty points wins the game.

Twenty Questions

Any number of people can play this famous guessing game. Start it by thinking of an object, anything at all, as long as other people have heard of it. It must fit into one of three categories: animal, vegetable, or mineral. When you are ready say so, and the questions can begin. Suppose you are thinking of a snapping turtle. The first questioner will ask, "Is it animal, vegetable, or mineral?" You must answer truthfully, "Animal." But you must answer all the other questions only by saying "Yes" or "No." The next question might be, "Does it walk on four feet?" "Yes," is of course the answer. The players take turns asking questions until they either guess the object or use up the 20 questions. If they cannot guess, tell them what it is and take another turn. If someone guesses correctly, he is **IT** and selects a new thing to be guessed for the next game.

OYSTER CLOISTER

MUT HUT

AWFUL JAWFULL

Hink Pink

What does a Big Wig have in common with a Brown Gown? What does an Inky Pinky have in common with Yellow Jello? All are pairs of rhyming words that could be used to play the game Hink Pink. The words in the pair must rhyme, have the same number of syllables, and describe something. If the words have two syllables, the pair is called a Hinky Pinky and three syllables make a Hinkety Pinkety. To start the game, a player thinks of a Hink Pink. He then thinks of a clue to give the other players who must guess

WHALE JAIL

HUMAN ZOOMIN

BUG HUG

APE CAPE

what the Hink Pink is. For example, you may say, "My Hink Pink is a large sloppy animal that loves to eat and roll in the mud." In this case, the Hink Pink is a Big Pig. Hink Pinks can be real or imaginary, as long as the clue allows the others to guess the answer. If your Hinky Pinky is Dragon Wagon, the clue might be, "My Hinky Pinky is a vehicle used to transport a mythological beast." The person who guesses correctly thinks of the next Hink Pink.

Buzz

Sometime or other, everyone learns how to play Buzz. It is a counting game and any number of people from 7 to 107 can play. It is easy to play, but pay attention, because it is just as easy to make a mistake. Everyone sits in a circle and someone begins the counting by saying "One." The next person says "Two," the next says "Three." The counting continues around the circle over and over, with each player saying the next higher number when it is his turn. But, whenever the number 7, or any number containing 7, or any multiple of 7, occurs, the player whose turn it is must say "Buzz" instead of the number. Anyone who says the number instead of "Buzz" is out. You may be wise to brush up on your multiplication before you begin. The last one out wins.

1 2 3 4 5 6 Buzz 8 9 10 11 12 13 Buzz 15 16 Buzz 18 19 20 Buzz 22 23 24 25 26 Buzz Buzz 29 30 31 32 33 etc. If you reach the 70s, say "Buzz-one" for 71 and so on. Can you guess what to say for 77? "Buzz-buzz," of course. And 107 is "One Hundred and Buzz."